Planning and Managing Change

INTRODUCING THE SERIES

Management Action Guides consists of a series of books written in an Open Learning style which are designed to be

- user friendly
- job related

Open Learning text is written in language which is easy to understand and avoids the use of jargon that is usually a feature of management studies. The text is interactive and is interspersed with Action Point questions to encourage the reader to apply the ideas from the text to their own particular situation at work. Space has been left after each Action Point question where responses can be written.

The Management Action Guides series will appeal to people who are already employed in a supervisory or managerial position and are looking to root their practical experience within more formal management studies.

Although Management Action Guides is a series of books that cover all aspects of management education, each book is designed to be free standing and does not assume that the reader has worked through any other book in the series.

Titles in The Management Action Guides series are

Planning and Managing Change

MANCHESTER
O·P·E·N
LEARNING

KOGAN
PAGE

First published in 1992 as *Managing Change* by Manchester Open Learning, Lower Hardman Street, Manchester M3 3FP

This edition published in 1993 by Kogan Page Ltd

Kogan Page Limited
120 Pentonville Road
London N1 9JN

British Library Cataloguing in Publication Data

A CIP record for this book is available from the British Library.

ISBN 0 7494 1143 0 (pb)
ISBN 0 7494 1336 0 (hb)

Printed and bound in Great Britain by Biddles Ltd, Guildford and Kings Lynn

Contents

GENERAL INTRODUCTION

'Nothing is permanent but change' Heraclitus (500 BC)

Change is part of our everyday life both at home and at work. The pace of change has increased dramatically in recent years and shows every sign of continuing to do so. To be a successful manager therefore means

■ to be able to accept change as a constant feature of life

■ to understand its effects on organisations and staff

■ to be able to identify the need for change

■ to be competent at planning, implementing and evaluating change

This book is designed to develop your knowledge and skills in those areas which promote successful management of change. Its main aims are for you to be able to

■ understand the need for change in your workplace

■ understand the effects of change on yourself and your team

■ lead and support your team in implementing change

The book starts by giving you a greater understanding of the pressures for change and of the factors which resist change. It is the balance between these two which will determine how quickly and successfully change can be introduced.

We then look at the relationship between change and the organisation, and between change and the individual.

An understanding of these areas enables us finally to look at change and the manager. That is to say, we look at your role not simply of coping with change, but also of actively leading your team in implementing change and achieving your organisational objectives.

1 PRESSURES FOR AND AGAINST CHANGE

Because of the increasingly globalised and deregulated environment in which modern business takes place, we are all subject to strong competitive pressures. These and other pressures oblige us to change the ways in which we operate from time to time. On the other hand, these necessary changes may be resisted by other pressures arising out of organisational or human factors within the company. Staff can sometimes fear the unknown consequences of change, for example, or the organisational structure of parts of an organisation may be incapable of or inconsistent with rapid change.

In this chapter we will be looking at the stages in the process of change, the pressure for change and the resistance to change.

1.1 THE PROCESS OF CHANGE

There are very few jobs that remain untouched by change for any considerable period of time. This is true of all industries at most times but is particularly true of the more successful, expanding businesses at a time, such as the last 15 to 20 years (and the foreseeable future), when advances in technology and other radical changes to the industrial context have occurred.

The change process can be seen as having 4 distinct stages. These are

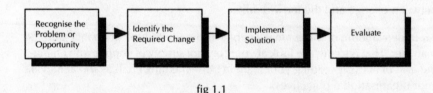

fig 1.1

We will now examine each of these stages in detail.

Recognising the Need for Change

Often in work situations it is a problem that makes us aware of the need for change. Perhaps we are losing business to competitors, or perhaps the office is no longer large enough.

At other times, change can result from an opportunity rather than from a problem. Computer technology may give us the opportunity to do a job more easily, for example.

ACTION POINT 1

Describe one problem and one opportunity which you have recently identified in your work area.

Identifying the Required Change

Once the need for change is recognised, we have to analyse the situation in more detail, examine alternative solutions and decide what changes we are going to make.

ACTION POINT 2

Make some notes of analysis on the problem and the opportunity described in Action Point 1. Describe the required changes, whether or not you have already implemented your solutions in real life.

Implementing the Change

In implementing change, we may have to change employee attitudes as well as changing, say, an administrative procedure.

We shall look at this critical aspect of change in detail in Chapter 3 of this book.

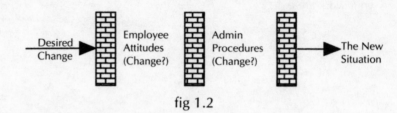

fig 1.2

Evaluating Change

It is important to monitor change closely to ensure that the desired outcome is achieved. We must also be on the look-out for unexpected 'side effects' which we may not have anticipated.

As a manager you will probably be more concerned with implementing change and evaluating it. You should also be constantly aware of problems and opportunities within the work that you are responsible for, and be prepared to make appropriate suggestions to senior managers if you believe that change is required.

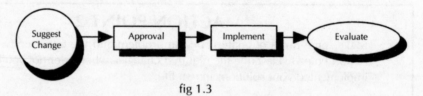

fig 1.3

ACTION POINT 3

In your own job, what changes have taken place since you started? Think of three examples which are as different as possible.

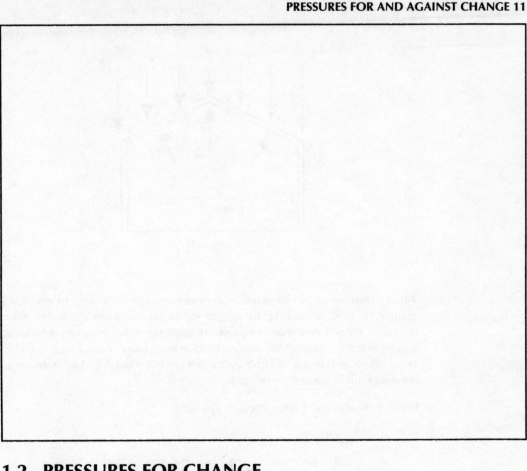

1.2   PRESSURES FOR CHANGE

We will now go on to look at the full range of factors which put pressure on organisations to change. Pressures for change can be both internal and external to the organisation.

Internal pressures can be

■   dissatisfaction with the present way of working

■   a desire to improve effectiveness

External pressures come from a variety of areas and are often the most significant factors in promoting change. We have already touched briefly on some of these factors and will now look at a more comprehensive list, containing seven sources of pressure.

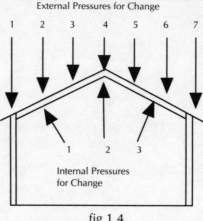

fig 1.4

These pressures all act to make us consider changing the way in which we operate. It is worth noting, though, that not all pressures act in the same direction. Indeed they may often oppose each other. For example, economic and technical pressures may suggest that we have more roads, larger vehicles, more intensive farming or faster trains, but environmental and perhaps social pressures might oppose these ideas.

Let us look at each of these pressures in turn.

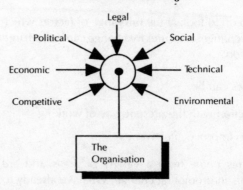

fig 1.5

(1) Legal Change

Industry is subject to legal restrictions locally, nationally and internationally (within the European arena and beyond), and changes in laws and regulations can come along at any time and affect issues at all levels.

ACTION POINT 4

Think of as many areas as possible where changes in the law will lead to changes at work, then think of as many sources of those changes as possible. Write down your suggestions in two lists in the space provided. Do not go into minute detail, but rather look at overall areas (such as Health and Safety) and categories of sources (such as the Department of Employment).

When you have completed your lists, compare them with those suggested over the page.

Here are some of the main areas you should have thought of. Possible sources are listed in brackets.

- Health and Safety legislation (EC Commission)
- Equal Opportunities (National Government [Dept of Employment, Environment, Health etc])
- Maternity (Local Bylaws)
- Other Employment Matters (Professional or Trade Association regulations [not legally binding but with de facto force])
- Factories Acts
- Environmental (pollution, noise etc)

It seems that almost any change in the law will have some effect on the way a company operates.

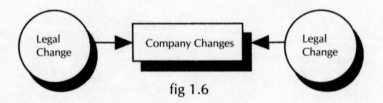

fig 1.6

(2) Technical Change

Technology is changing at an amazing rate. Some would say an alarming rate. It is estimated that 90% of the scientists who ever lived are alive today, and that our store of knowledge doubles every 15 years.

Technology presents us with many opportunities: the microcomputer, medical scanners and fibre optics are just three examples of major steps forward in industry and society as a result of technological development.

ACTION POINT 5

Taking the computer as the most common example of technological advance in recent years, think of as many key areas as you can where your company is using computers and list them in the space provided.

Compare your lists with the suggestions of a colleague and add to your list if necessary.

The rate of technical change is increasing all the time. This leads to shorter product life cycles. In turn, this means that staff will be adapting more often to new equipment.

ACTION POINT 6

In the space provided, list any items of equipment which you use which have changed in any way since you joined the company.

When you have completed this Action Point, discuss your answers with a work colleague.

(3) Economic Change

Changes in our own and other economies can have a profound effect on the operation of any industry.

Some changes will impact on all industries to greater or lesser extent, while others will have an impact restricted to certain specific areas of business.

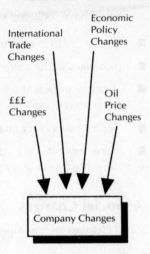

fig 1.7

ACTION POINT 7

What kinds of economic changes are likely to have an impact on all industries? Think of as many as you can (illustrating them with actual examples where they exist) and list them in the space provided. Compare your ideas with the text that follows.

You could have included such things as

- a rise or fall in raw material prices (eg. the rises in oil prices since 1973)
- changes in the pattern of international trade
- currency fluctuations (and the effects on prices of imported materials and exported goods)
- economic policy changes (import controls, for example)
- new markets (the advent of new markets abroad through the rise of income levels or removal of trade barriers)

(4) Social Changes

Social changes are an important influence on business, for two main reasons.

Firstly, customer expectations change - and almost always in an upward direction. Higher standards of product quality, choice and availability are constantly demanded as is an increasing level of personal customer care. Paradoxically, as industrial and service units become bigger and more globally active the customer tends to develop a requirement for more personalised, individual treatment.

Secondly, employee expectations change. You may expect to have your boss relate to you in a less formal, hierarchical manner, or to have child-minding facilities available, or to have longer holidays.

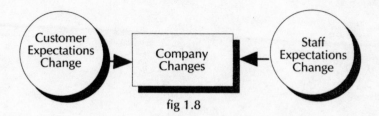

fig 1.8

ACTION POINT 8

List at least three ways (for each) in which you believe customer expectations and employee expectations are changing within your industry sector.

(5) Political Change

All industries, to some extent, are susceptible to political changes, most but not all of which manifest themselves in economic terms. A prime example of this was the enormous impact on industry caused by the sharp increase in the price of oil in the mid 1970s which was, in turn, caused by political changes in the oil producing countries.

Political changes, interpreted broadly (and in international as well as domestic terms) can impact on business in all kinds of ways.

ACTION POINT 9

List at least three actual or possible ways in which industry can be susceptible to political changes at home or abroad.

Compare your answers with ours as you continue reading the text.

You may have thought of examples similar to the following

- regional policy - fluctuations in government policy on attracting investment to one part of the country or another. This can affect several kinds of business decisions - investment, moving location, transportation and so on

- diplomatic changes - changes in relations between the UK and other nations, affecting import and export possibilities

- taxation - changes in the burden of taxation in the Chancellor's budget or other economic statements

- purchasing - political controls (or economic influences created by the state) influencing an industry's choice of sources of materials

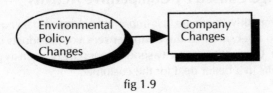

fig 1.9

(6) Environmental Change

There is a rapidly growing awareness of environmental issues - and a consequent pressure on industry, either directly or through Government agencies, to take them into account when making business decisions. In many cases these have even led some firms actively to gear themselves and promote themselves as environmentally aware and caring companies. Few firms can now disregard environmental issues at no cost to their customer image and, ultimately, to sales figures.

ACTION POINT 10

Think of at least 4 environmental issues that have an impact on industry today - 2 general ones and 2 from your own industry sector.

General and 'high profile' environmental issues affecting industry at present include

- lead-free petrol - the effects on the petrochemical and car manufacturing industries

- CFCs - the effect on consumer goods industries (refrigerators, aerosols etc) of the perceived effect on the ozone layer of chlorofluorocarbons

- Green Belt - protection of rural and suburban land around cities and towns against incursion by development (dwellings and 'green field' sites for industry)

- water and air pollution - changes in production and waste processes to lessen environmental damage (by local or national law)

(7) Change Caused by Competitive Activity

In a highly competitive business, it is important to know what your competitors are doing, and to ensure that the customer sees your products or services as being the best. Competitive activity should generally be seen as good, since it normally results in a better deal for the customer.

Price is obviously an important element in competitive strategy, but the level and type of service and quality of product offered are becoming increasingly important.

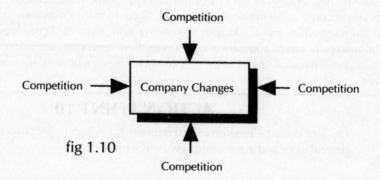

fig 1.10

ACTION POINT 11

List at least two instances where competitive activity has led to alterations in the products or services (or method of delivery of those) within your firm, or where competitors have introduced changes as a result of the company's new developments. Explain each one briefly.

1.3   RESISTANCE TO CHANGE

Just as there are forces pressuring for change, so there are forces resisting it.

In customer-led companies, change will almost always be in the customer's interest. Nonetheless, all change is unsettling, even to those who stand to benefit most from it, and it is sometimes possible that some customers may initially be unhappy with some changes.

Most resistance to change will come from either the structure of the organisation itself, or from managers or other individuals within the organisation.

The reasons why this resistance occurs, and how it can be handled successfully, will be examined in more detail in subsequent chapters. The types of resistance we can typically expect are shown in the diagram and are discussed in the text which follows.

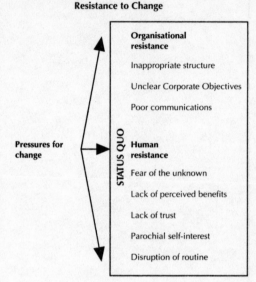

fig 1.11

ACTION POINT 12

Describe one change you were responsible for introducing at some time in your working life and the resistance you encountered. Specify the source(s) of the resistance.

Let's now examine each of the sources of resistance in turn.

(1) Inappropriate Structure

While some organisations have structures which are able to adapt quickly to new circumstances, others are very resistant to change. Some of these structural problems are

■ a 'tall' management structure with lots of levels of control

■ a very large organisation

■ not much delegation of authority

■ a large number of rules

■ poor communications

These are some of the features of what we normally call a bureaucratic structure where authority, the rule book and time honoured practice are the norms rather than initiative, innovation and flexible responses.

(2) Unclear Corporate Objectives

When corporate objectives or goals are unclear, then different managers can be working in different directions, each thinking that they are doing what is in the company's interests.

Where company objectives are clearly stated and understood, then managers will know what direction they are to work in. This way, all effort should be constructive, and it should be apparent from the objectives whether a particular change is desirable or not.

(3) Poor Communications

Poor communications will make it harder to bring about change. When you are planning change you must ensure that the right information gets to the right people at the right time.

ACTION POINT 13

How could you make sure that you had communicated the same instruction to five people in exactly the same way?

You probably suggested writing the instruction down and sending file copies. So far, so good. But you also need to ensure that all employees have received your memorandum and understood it. This is best done by talking to each person, where possible, and checking out their understanding, and encouraging any comments or questions.

(4) Human Factors

Not everyone will display all of the reactions to change which we looked at earlier. However, it would be surprising if these factors were not present in some measure.

So far we have looked at pressures for change, and resistance which acts against change.

Let us now combine the diagrams we have used so far.

Resistance to Pressures

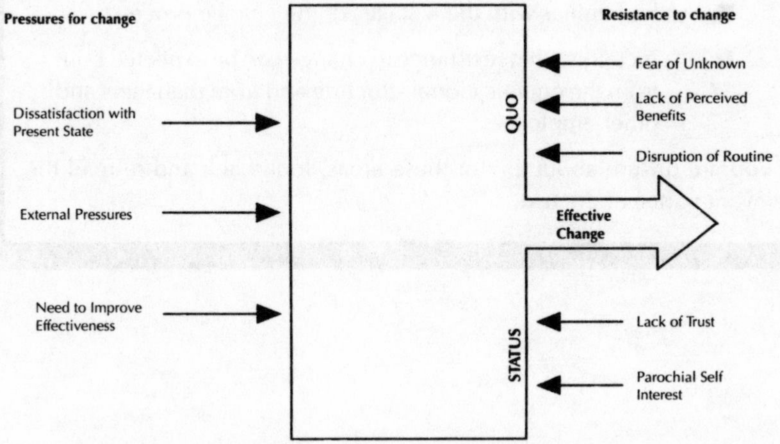

Pressures for change		Resistance to change
		Fear of Unknown
Dissatisfaction with Present State	QUO	Lack of Perceived Benefits
		Disruption of Routine
External Pressures	Effective Change	
Need to Improve Effectiveness	STATUS	Lack of Trust
		Parochial Self Interest

fig 1.12

For effective change to take place, the status quo has to change. That is where your skill as a manager comes in.

There will be many specific ways in which you can help to move the status quo in the direction of effective change by using your managerial skills as a positive pressure for change. But in brief general terms most of these will come under

- increasing your staff's awareness of the external and internal pressures for change, and how these pressures fit in with corporate objectives

- encouraging individuals to lower their resistance to changes by

  - creating an atmosphere of trust

  - making them aware of longer term benefits to themselves

CHAPTER SUMMARY

After completing this chapter you should now

- be aware that change is a response to many pressures

- understand that these pressures can act in combination with each other, or can oppose each other

- realise that the ever growing rate of technical change is a strong pressure for other change, especially in combination with competitive activity

- be familiar with the 4 stages of the change process

- recognise that resistance to change can be expected both from the organisational structure and from managers and other employees

If you are unsure about any of these areas, look back and re-read the relevant part(s) of the text.

2 CHANGE AND ORGANISATION STRUCTURE

Having analysed the pressures towards and against organisational change, we must now take a closer look at the structure of organisations.

Organisations exist when tasks that are to be performed involve more than one person. The organisation provides a structure which links the jobs together into a workflow system. It also provides control and co-ordination of the workflow.

When changes occur in the environment in which an organisation operates, then that organisation has to change to remain healthy and competitive.

The ability of an organisation to adapt to change will depend very much on its structure. But organisations differ greatly in their structures, and indeed different parts of the same organisation may be structured differently.

In this chapter we will look at organisation structure and change, the breakdown into mechanistic and organic organisation types, the structure of your company, and future trends in organisation development.

2.1 STRUCTURING ORGANISATIONS

What do we mean by structure? In his book entitled 'Organisation', John Child identifies six major dimensions of an organisation's structure

1   The allocation of tasks and responsibilities to individuals

2   The designation of formal reporting relationships. This sets the number of levels in hierarchies, and determines the span of control of managers and managers

3   The design of systems to ensure effective communication of information, integration of effort, and participation in the decision making process

4   The delegation of authority, along with a system to monitor and evaluate the use of discretion

5   The grouping together of individuals in sections or departments, grouping of departments within divisions, and of divisions within the organisation

Grouping Individuals

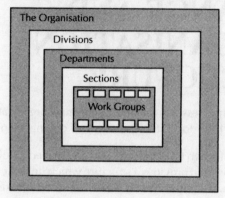

fig 2.1

6   The provision of systems for performance appraisal and reward which help to motivate rather than to alienate employees

2.2 MECHANISTIC AND ORGANIC STRUCTURES

We will now look at two types of structure, which can be thought of as extremes. Most organisations will contain elements of both types.

The two types are often labelled as

■   mechanistic

■   organic

These terms are used by Burns and Stalker in 'The Management of Innovation'.

In a mechanistic organisation you would expect to find

■   all major decisions being taken at the top

■   a clear, rigid, vertical reporting structure

■   information flowing downwards

■   jobs compartmentalised, with very clear and limiting job descriptions

■   managers staying in one specialism during their career, only becoming involved in other functions at the most senior levels

■   a high level of conformity expected from staff

The Mechanistic Organisation

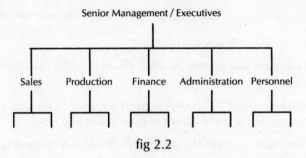

fig 2.2

ACTION POINT 14

What elements of your company could make you think it is a mechanistic organisation?

The Organic Organisation

The organic organisation provides a sharp contrast to the mechanistic structure

■ there are fewer 'levels of command'

■ decisions are devolved to the lowest level at which they can sensibly be taken

■ information flows in all directions as required, with consultation and discussion being more common than orders and directives

■ job descriptions tend to be written in terms of objectives or targets rather than tasks

■ managers will often be encouraged to gain as broad an experience of the organisation as possible, and a typical career would involve a number of 'development' moves

■ innovation and suggestion are encouraged

Drawing a chart for an organic organisation is often difficult, as there are so many different lines of reporting, consultation and liaison. But one type often found would be the matrix structure illustrated here.

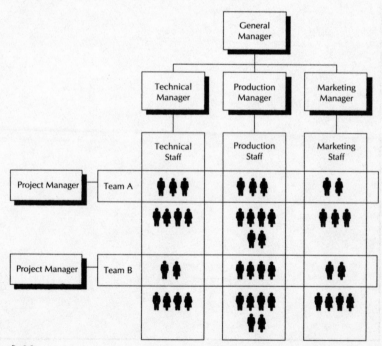

fig 2.3

An organic organisation may contain a number of matrix managers and supervisors: that is, managers or supervisors who have two bosses rather than one. An IT specialist may be responsible to a production, sales or other manager operationally but to the head of Information Technology Services (or whatever it may be called) professionally.

ACTION POINT 15

From the description given above, you may realise that you have already come across mechanistic and organic organisations under other names or terms. Write down any other terms which you would associate with each type of organisation.

Mechanistic organisations could also be characterised or labelled as

1   Bureaucratic

2   Authoritarian

3   Formal

4   Traditional

Organic organisations could also be described as

1   Democratic

2   Informal

3   Modern

It would be wrong to think of mechanistic organisations as necessarily bad, and organic ones as necessarily good. Each has its strengths and its weaknesses, which the next Action Point will illustrate. It is the suitability of an organisation's structure to its business activities that is important - and its ability to adapt to changing circumstances as rapidly as necessary if it is in a changing market or situation.

ACTION POINT 16

Decide which organisational structure would be best for each of the following tasks and explain briefly why you think this

1   A firm making and selling house bricks

2   A research and development department

3   An army

4   An advertising agency

5   A coal mine

6   An independent television company

For organisations 1, 3 and 5 a mechanistic structure is probably most appropriate.

In general these organisations perform routine tasks with little change, and with little need for consultation.

For organisations 2, 4 and 6 the tasks are irregular, often working to deadlines and with a high need to share information. Thus an organic structure seems more appropriate.

In many respects the two structures we have looked at represent opposite poles of organisation, while the structure which is most common in modern industry is known as Hierarchy.

Hierarchy

Hierarchy is the traditional organisation structure and takes the form of a pyramid format, through which a clear line of authority stretches from the lowest level to the highest.

Hierarchy can be shown diagrammatically as a series of job positions linked together by authority and accountability and in general, the more levels there are in the hierarchy, the more lengthy and difficult communication becomes, as we have seen from fig. 2.2 on page 31.

It is worth mentioning here that as well as the communication difficulties arising from increasing the number of levels in a hierarchy, it has generally been considered that a manager or supervisor must have a limit to the number of people whom he or she can supervise effectively; the rule which is often quoted is that the number of people supervised by one individual should be kept to a minimum and that in general that number should be four to seven.

This size of chapter and number of staff managed is often referred to as the span of control.

In fact, however, where the company culture and organisation encourage the sharing of responsibility, and give autonomy to individuals and groups through training and delegation, and where they create a strong team culture which empowers staff to use their talents and initiative fully for the common goals, it is quite possible for one manager to be in charge of far greater numbers, as Japanese practice shows.

ACTION POINT 17

Describe the structure of your department using the 6 dimensions discussed at the beginning of this chapter.

In designing large organisations, there is normally a need to compromise between

■ the number of levels of hierarchy and

■ the span of control

An organisation with a large number of levels in the hierarchy is labelled tall, while a small number of levels is labelled flat.

Very tall organisations are seen to be bureaucratic and slow to respond to change. However, if you have only a few levels between the top and bottom of an organisation, then managers and supervisors will each have a high number of employees to supervise, which is not always desirable either. Each model has its negative side. For example, 'flatter' structures, although usually associated with faster moving, more responsive organisations, also bring with them certain drawbacks, including the need for managers to receive (and so understand and act upon) a large number of reports from diverse sections of the company. This clearly has implications for the attitudes, and calibre required for management in such companies.

These design choices lead to a wide variety of organisational structures in practice.

ACTION POINT 18

Think of the an organisation of roughly the same size (in terms of personnel) as your company, then consider that organisation and the company under dimension 2 above (formal reporting relationships). Is your company more or less 'tall' than the other organisation?

2.3   THE STRUCTURE OF YOUR COMPANY

Let us now think about the structure of your own company.

You may find it helpful at this point to obtain any available company organisation charts which show the overall structure of the whole company, the structure and interrelationships of different functions or departments within the company, your own department or section's organisation chart and so on.

ACTION POINT 19

Can you think of any parts or aspects of the structure of your company which you would see as either mechanistic and organic in structure? Do you see these as relating to questions of stability and change in any way?

Your answer will probably have identified some of the central and operational structures as having hierarchical and mechanistic features, but with an overlaid matrix element of cross departmental functions and accountabilities that gives them the organic capability for flexible response and rapid change. It also allows the setting up of special project teams or other dedicated work groups.

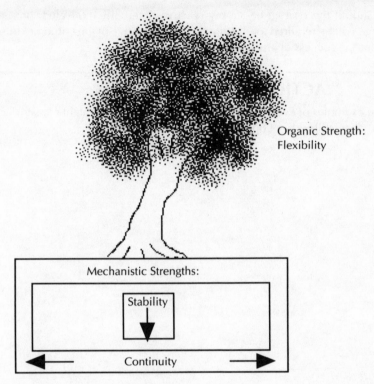

Organic Strength:
Flexibility

Mechanistic Strengths:

Stability

Continuity

fig 2.4

The conclusion which you may well have reached is that an organisation needs to be organic, at least in part, if it is to be able to respond quickly to change, and it needs to develop managers and staff who can accept change as a natural part of their working lives.

At the same time, it is essential to have sufficient stability and continuity to enable operations to continue normally. This suggests that much of the work of an organisation may still take place in mechanistic structures.

Business survival increasingly depends on an organisation's ability to respond to change. Organisations may have to be prepared to change

■ systems

■ structures

■ policies

in order to remain truly competitive.

Nor should the change be simply reactive. Internally motivated, pro-active change will be required for the effective performance of the corporate mission and for the success of any organisation.

ACTION POINT 20

Give at least three examples of events and business decisions which might cause an organisation to change its way of operating.

Examples of events which might cause an organisation to change are

- acquiring or merging with another company
- introducing a new service or product
- national or international competition
- new technology

2.4 ORGANISATIONS OF THE FUTURE

What does the future hold for organisations? We can make a number of predictions.

1   Multi-national organisations seem likely to continue to grow, within legal constraints

2   External pressures will continue to demand responsive organisations, with a general trend for organisations to become more organic

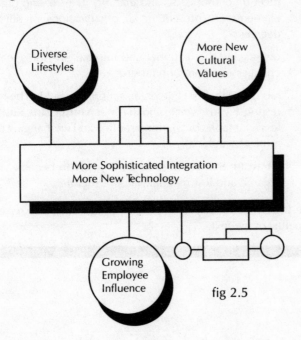

fig 2.5

3   More complex and diverse activities will lead to a need for more sophisticated integration and co-ordination. However, technology can be expected to assist greatly in this

4   There will be greater diversity of lifestyles of both customers and employees with a need to adapt to an increasing range of cultural values

5   Employees at all levels will have more influence, with power being shared more equally

CHAPTER SUMMARY

After completing this chapter you should now

■ know the major dimensions of organisation structure

■ know the main features of mechanistic and organic structures

■ recognise that different types of organisation structure meet different needs, and that mechanistic and organic elements are present in all organisations in differing degrees

■ understand that external and internal pressures lead to changes in organisational structure

■ recognise that organic organisations are held to be more responsive to change, and that mechanistic structures are less adaptable, but perform routine and unchanging tasks more economically

■ be aware that organisations are likely to become more organic and less mechanistic in structure

If you are unsure about any of these areas, look back and re-read the relevant part(s) of the text.

3 CHANGE AND THE INDIVIDUAL

Organisational change will often require individuals to change not only their behaviour, but also their attitudes.

Individuals vary in their approach to change. But it is completely natural to resist change and to find it stressful. People will usually see the disadvantages of the new more clearly than the benefits. Conversely, they will usually overvalue the comfort of the habitual and familiar ways of doing things.

This suggests that people need to be supported through change. The more extreme the change the more support they will need.

Extreme change can be overwhelming if the individual is not properly supported.

In this chapter we will look at human responses to change, the relationship between change, learning and stress and the individual's transition over time from the old situation to the new.

3.1 INSECURITY AND FEAR

Individuals can experience either evolutionary or revolutionary change.

An example of evolutionary change is the ageing process. Because this happens a little each day, we are almost unaware of the change, and can accept it.

Revolutionary change, on the other hand, is much harder for an individual to accept, and can often be met with strong resistance.

Change threatens individuals at the security level, and indeed may even threaten their survival within an organisation if redundancy is a real option.

The human resistance to change which we looked at in Chapter One of this book are found in each of us to a greater or lesser extent.

Fear of the unknown is something we are all familiar with. If we are blindfolded we will walk much more cautiously, even when we know that we are on a smooth path. Equally, we are expected to feel some fear the first time that we fly, swim, ride a bicycle and so on.

Of course, something is only truly unknown once. As we repeat an activity, our initial fear is reduced.

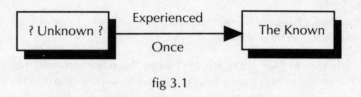

fig 3.1

ACTION POINT 21

List at least three times in your life when you have experienced fear of the unknown, and gone on to overcome it.

Is there anything which fear of the unknown still stops you from doing?

3.2 CHANGE, LEARNING AND STRESS

It does not have to be a physical activity which causes fear. Often people doubt their ability to learn a new way of thinking about something.

When we learn something new, we go through a number of stages. These can be described as

(1) Unconscious Ignorance

This is where we can't do something, but don't even know we can't do it. We might have had this attitude to car driving before we even considered learning.

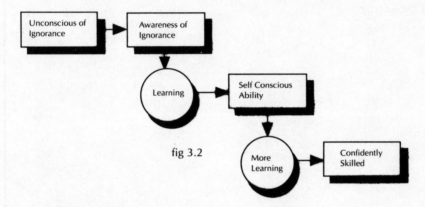

fig 3.2

(2) Conscious Ignorance

This is where we decide to learn to drive, and suddenly become aware of all the things we don't know and can't do.

(3) Conscious Knowledge

We have started to drive, but have to think carefully about everything, such as what gear to be in, where to position the car, how hard to press the accelerator, where to look and soon.

(4) Unconscious Knowledge

Driving has now become second nature. We don't think about it. We just get into the car and it happens.

The whole process might be summed up as in the diagram above.

Unconscious knowledge, like unconscious ignorance, causes no stress. It is the change between the two that causes difficulty. Indeed, the stress of conscious ignorance, or conscious knowledge, may be so demanding that we decide to give up rather than trying to manage the stress which continuing would involve.

Change without stress is seldom possible. But we can develop ways of reducing the stress, or at least making it more bearable. Fear of the unknown can be overcome.

ACTION POINT 22

Think back to a recent major learning experience in your life. Try to remember and express the feelings you went through between unconscious ignorance and unconscious knowledge.

3.3 BENEFITS, ROUTINE AND TRUST

Another reason for not wanting to change is a lack of perceived benefits. Why should anything change? What will be the benefit to me, or to the customer, or to the company?

ACTION POINT 23

Imagine that you work as an enquiry manager. You are told to keep a record of every enquiry, which you have not had to do before.

1   What reaction do you expect from your staff?

2   What could you do to overcome the lack of perceived benefits?

---

1   You could expect these forms of resistance

■   questioning why

■   avoidance of new work

■   poor completion of new work

■   poor morale and lack of motivation

■   recruiting other staff to support their resistance

2   You could overcome this resistance by

■   discussing the benefits to the company with your staff in terms of a better understanding of customer needs, leading to improvements in service, higher turnover, more secure and better paid jobs

■   finding some improvement to compensate for the extra work

■   setting an example in keeping the records and making constructive use of them

Disruption of routine can also cause resistance to change. Any new way of working will take more effort and time at first, even if it is much easier in the long run. This process, whereby the time and effort involved in mastering the new activity gradually decreases, is known as the learning curve and is shown graphically below.

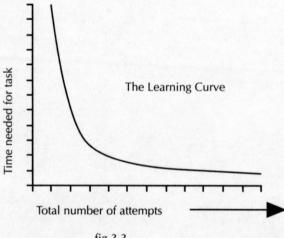

fig 3.3

Eventually, the old routine will be forgotten, and the new way of working will have become the new routine. But the stress of making the transition will be reduced if managers recognise that staff will be slower and more prone to error while they are learning.

Finally, it is not unusual for staff to exhibit a lack of trust when changes are being introduced.

Factors leading to this mistrust might include

- a general belief that management are 'up to something'
- in a badly run company, there may be a history of exploitative changes, or redundancies
- a lack of frankness, trust, communication, consultation and concern for its people in the previous record of the company

The possible consequences could be that the change will not be implemented, or only partially implemented, which would be very serious if the change were needed for the survival of the firm. Industrial action could also not be ruled out.

3.4 HANDLING INDIVIDUAL RESISTANCE TO CHANGE

The importance of trust can never be overstated. Most of the human factors resisting change can be overcome by

- openness
- talking things through

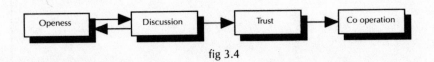

fig 3.4

And clearly the greater the degree of openness and trust that a Manager or Supervisor has already fostered within the team, the easier this process will be.

With parochial self interest, however, the problem is one of the person's attitude rather than knowledge. Self interest is understandable, but sooner or later the person will have to see that their position must change. In the publishing industry, for example, typesetting and printing technology changes, fiercely and long resisted, have nevertheless come about.

We have been looking at the ways in which 'the average person' normally resists change. However, not everyone will resist in the same way or to the same degree. Indeed, many changes will be welcomed by staff who see them as providing opportunities for career progression, or job enhancement.

To what extent will individual responses to change vary? The next Action Point will encourage you to think of what variables within the individual are important.

ACTION POINT 24

In your opinion what differences between individuals will make them respond differently to change?

3.5 INDIVIDUAL ATTITUDES TO CHANGE

A number of variables are considered important in determining a person's attitude to change. These include

■ social characteristics

■ personality

■ personal goals

■ job attitudes

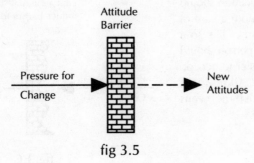

fig 3.5

Social Characteristics

What social characteristics are important? Perhaps the most important would be

(a) age

(b) social and economic position

(c) education

ACTION POINT 25

In what way would you expect each of the social characteristic to alter a person's attitude to change?

It is dangerous to generalise. However, it is probable that an older person will find it harder to change, as habits have had longer to become established, and also the history of change (with its relatively recent acceleration) means that many older people still do not see it as a necessary part of life.

Social and economic position nowadays is frequently discussed in terms of different 'lifestyles', instead of 'class'. Resistance to change is probably greatest where the lifestyle is most conservative, which would be at the extremes of the social scale.

And finally, education should make people more aware of change as a part of life, so a more educated person should find change easier to accept, though this, like most generalisations, is by no means always the case.

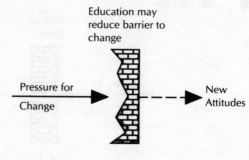

fig 3.6

Personality

Important personality factors which affect our readiness to meet change are

(a)   our adaptability or rigidity of nature and outlook

(b)   our security needs (people who are insecure or less secure than they would like to be tend to be less adaptable)

(c)   the values that are important to us as individuals

Personal Goals

An individual's own goals are important. Whether they seek satisfaction of their needs inside or outside the organisation will be an important factor also.

Job Attitudes

Job attitudes will also be important. Someone who sees the need for change will probably support it, as long as it supports their own position rather than undermining it. Someone of long work experience in a particular job, however, may take the attitude that change is a criticism of their past performance and is to be resisted.

Summing Up

It should be increasingly clear that individuals respond in different ways to change, and that a wide variety of personal factors come into play. The implication of this for the manager is that where resistance is encountered, an understanding of the individual and of their needs will be important in deciding how to overcome the resistance to change.

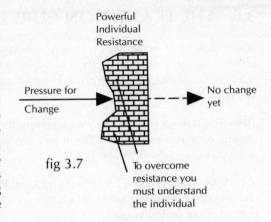

Powerful Individual Resistance

Pressure for Change

No change yet

fig 3.7

To overcome resistance you must understand the individual

ACTION POINT 26

For at least two people who work for you, estimate how well or how badly you expect them to react to change. Then, referring to the characteristics discussed here, write down the individual factors which could cause them to react in the way that you envisage.

3.6   THE TRANSITION CURVE

The responses of individuals will vary considerably not only from person to person, but also over time. By this we mean that a person will respond negatively to a change at one point, but perhaps have a different attitude to it at a later stage.

There is a pattern to this, and we can graph the response of an individual to change over a period of time. Obviously the more traumatic the change, the more pronounced will be the effect.

In their book 'Transitions', Adams, Hayes and Hopson show that major work changes can resemble other major changes, such as bereavement or marriage, in their effect on individuals.

They believe that people going through such change progress through seven stages

- immobilisation
- denial of change
- incompetence
- acceptance of reality
- testing possibilities
- search for meaning
- integration

The time taken to accept major changes fully can be as much as 18 months or even longer. However, an understanding of what is happening can often reduce the time needed to come to terms with change, and to fully adopt new ways of behaving. (A manager's support and concern through the stages will also be critical for the individual team member faced with major change. Understanding of the process will also help the manager to deal with the individual in a way appropriate to the stage they are at.)

This process is best understood graphically, when it is known as The Transition Curve (see fig 3.8). This curve shows how competence varies with time and it reflects the likely changes of mood and morale (as well as the development of competence) in its progress.

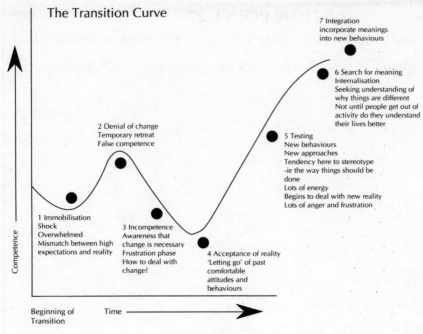

The Transition Curve

7 Integration
incorporate meanings
into new behaviours

6 Search for meaning
Internalisation
Seeking understanding of
why things are different
Not until people get out of
activity do they understand
their lives better

2 Denial of change
Temporary retreat
False competence

5 Testing
New behaviours
New approaches
Tendency here to stereotype
-ie the way things should be
done
Lots of energy
Begins to deal with new reality
Lots of anger and frustration

1 Immobilisation
Shock
Overwhelmed
Mismatch between high
expectations and reality

3 Incompetence
Awareness that
change is necessary
Frustration phase
How to deal with
change?

4 Acceptance of reality
'Letting go' of past
comfortable
attitudes and
behaviours

Competence

Beginning of
Transition

Time

fig 3.8

3.7   THE WORKER AND THE ORGANISATION

In the first two chapters of this book, we examined the pressures for change, mainly external, and the relationship between change and the organisation.

So far we have looked at forms of resistance to change which people exhibit, and how this can relate to individual characteristics.

In the next chapter we shall examine the role of the manager in managing change.

This should be easier to look at now that we have studied the relationship between change and the organisation, and the relationship between change and the individual.

But what of the relationship between the organisation and the individual? There is often a considerable gap between what the worker expects from the organisation, and what the organisation expects from the worker.

ACTION POINT 27

Note at least four things that you think the worker expects from the organisation.

Then, note at least four things that you think the organisation expects from the worker.

Interesting, isn't it? Once job and basic financial security are satisfied, the worker expects the organisation to meet higher level needs and motivators; whereas the organisation often expects predictable, routine behaviour from the worker.

A full comparison of expectations within many traditional, hierarchical organisations might well look something like the table on the next page.

Worker Expectations	Organisational Realities
Challenge and personal growth	Work is simple and repetitive
A democratic approach, with consultation	Tall hierarchies and long chains of command
Commitment influenced by the work itself	Emphasis on material rewards to staff
Participation, involvement, communication two way	Communication one-way; downwards
Joint work-planning and decision-making	Authority based structures
Career management and self development	Movement depends on organisational needs
Attitudes of mutual trust, respect and co-operation	Impersonal interaction between hierarchies

In such organisations the gap between individual aspirations and organisational realities is likely to have a demotivating effect and to adversely affect attitudes to and ability to cope with change. Which is one of the primary reasons why the most successful companies have tended to move significantly towards structures and cultures which will give autonomy and individual responsibility within their operational and budgetary constraints and involve their people through openness and consultation.

CHAPTER SUMMARY

After completing this chapter you should now

■ be aware that change for the individual can mean a change in attitude as well as a change in behaviour

■ understand that significant change can provoke resistance which may prevent the change from being effective

■ recognise that this resistance is a result of human responses and fears about change

■ be aware that traumatic changes will take some time to work through and become incorporated into new behaviours

■ see how an understanding of the transition curve will assist a manager in comprehending and dealing with this process

If you are unsure about any of there areas, look back and re-read the relevant part(s) of the text.

4 CHANGE AND THE MANAGER

The manager is a key figure in the introduction and management of change.

Managers have to be able to cope with change themselves as well as managing the work team through the difficulties of change.

They also have a secondary role in identifying changes that are required within their area of responsibility, and in introducing changes that are within their job remit.

In this chapter we will examine the role of the manager in managing change, the flow of information, and six strategies for handling resistance to change.

4.1 ADJUSTING TO CHANGE

When change affects your work team, you as a manager have first of all to cope with the change yourself. This is more difficult for you than for other members of the team for two reasons

1   Other team members can turn to you for support, whereas it will not always be practicable for you to turn to your manager for support

2   As a manager, you will face additional problems to those faced by your team

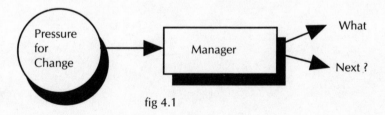

fig 4.1

Your additional problems might, for example, include any of the following possibilities

■ if the change is operational and must be rapidly introduced, you may have to take more of a 'Telling' style of management than you feel comfortable with

■ you may have to cope with a lot of complaints from your staff

■ a change might erode your own pay differential or status

■ you will be accountable to your manager if the change does not go smoothly

■ there may be an additional workload

■ you carry the responsibility for organising and implementing the change

As you can see, there is a lot more responsibility on your shoulders than on other team members. The pressure may well be to resolve any personal uncertainty about the change quickly, so that you can then devote all your effort to bringing about the change in your area of responsibility.

ACTION POINT 28

Think of a change you have implemented in your chapter or unit in the recent past.

1   Which of the additional problems listed above did you have to cope with? Were there any other additional problems not listed there?

2   What help is available to you in resolving personal uncertainty about change? (Check this out with your manager or with the Personnel Department).

4.2 THE ROLE OF THE MANAGER

So what is your role in bringing change about?

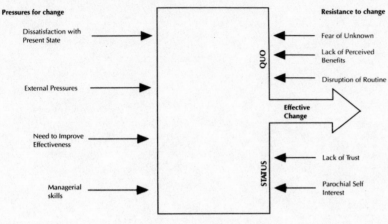

fig 4.2

You have seen this diagram before. You will remember that it shows on the one side the pressures for change, and on the other the forces which resist change.

In addition, we have now included the manager.

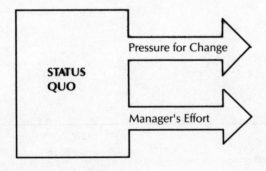

fig 4.3

ACTION POINT 29

Looking at the diagram, in what three ways do you think a manager can act to increase the effectiveness of change?

The manager can

■   act to reduce the factors opposing change

■   act to increase the pressures for change

■   be a pressure for change

You can be a force in the equation yourself, as well as being able to influence all the other factors that are operating.

The example you set as leader will be extremely important. People who work for you will look at your reaction first, before deciding whether to give their wholehearted co-operation to the change. If they see you doing so, they are much more likely to follow you. If you seem uncertain about the change, however, then they are likely to assume that you would prefer them to be unenthusiastic as well.

4.3 COMMUNICATION AND VISION

One of the other ways in which you will be influential is in making your team aware of the pressures for change, which you will probably much more readily recognise

- you can tell them what you know about the external pressures, such as competition, which are acting to bring the change about

- you can explain why managers, or customers, or others are dissatisfied with the status quo, and make them aware of the need to improve effectiveness

- you can communicate to your team the vision of where they can get to by responding positively to the need for change as an opportunity, putting it into the context of the corporate mission

Finally, you can help them to overcome their own fears and reservations, which stand between them and change.

ACTION POINT 30

In your opinion, when should you start to prepare your team for a change which you know is coming in a few months' time?

As with many managerial questions, there is no right or wrong answer. On the one hand it is important to make preparations comfortably in advance. On the other hand it is equally important to have staff using the present system properly. Avoid giving them the excuse that it is going to change anyway.

As the diagram below shows, failing to prepare for change means that the change comes as a sudden shock to the smooth flow of work.

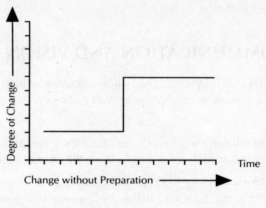

fig 4.4

Preparing for change in advance allows the transition to be much smoother. You will see from the second diagram that the change takes some time afterwards to be fully effective. That is quite realistic, corresponding to the learning curve described earlier.

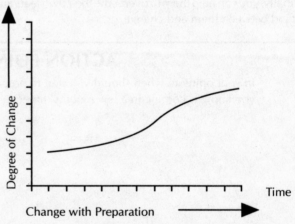

fig 4.5

4.4 ALWAYS PREPARED FOR CHANGE

There are a number of things you can do on a regular basis which will assist with the implementation of change

■ know your team individually, and know how they influence each other. Often you will only have to convince one or two people of the need to change, if you know that they are a positive influence on the others

■ communicate regularly with your team as a matter of course, and ensure that an atmosphere of trust exists within the team. Make sure you establish yourself as a manager who listens and cares for your people

■ be prepared to fight to ensure that the resources are available to allow the change to be brought in successfully and be ready to give every support to your team in the process

■ have established routines, which you will maintain through times of change. This may be something as simple as having coffee together, but the familiarity of routines is a good counterbalance to the uncertainty of change

If you incorporate these points into your day to day management style, then you should have a workgroup which will more readily respond to being led through change.

4.5 INITIATING CHANGE

Of course, not all change is externally imposed. Your company will expect you as a manager to take the initiative in bringing about changes to improve the work for which they are responsible.

When you identify a possible improvement, talk to your manager if necessary to gain agreement and support, or a further opinion, and talk to the team members involved, if the suggestion did not come from them.

Then think about it in relation to the stages of the change process.

The four stages in the process of change are

1   Recognising the need for change

2   Identifying the required change

-     from the real causes of problem

-     from the effects of the opportunity

3   Implement the change

4   Evaluate the change

Often you will be presented with a problem and a suggested solution at the same time. It is important to be able to distinguish between these, and to look at them separately.

Ask yourself

■   is the problem the real problem, or is it just a symptom of another problem?

■   will the solution being suggested solve the real problem?

■   will it have any other side effects?

■   is there another and better solution?

Always be prepared to ask the staff doing the job what they think of the problem. At the very least it will make them feel involved.

When implementing the change, always ensure that you have decided how you are going to evaluate it. You must be sure that you are achieving the effect you wanted. Ideally, you should monitor regularly during the change process, so that you can respond quickly if things do not go exactly as you predicted.

The sort of change that you will originate yourself will normally be in response to a problem. As well as dealing with problems, however, managers at all levels should be constantly aware of opportunities.

Again, the first question should be whether or not it is within your scope to act on the opportunity yourself, or whether you need to talk to your manager and get agreement and support for your decision.

A useful checklist for considering how to act on opportunities could be

Category	Definition	Notes
Ideals	What do I **want** to do?	
Requirements	What **should** I do?	
Constraints	What **must** I do?	
Limitations/ Resources	What **can** I do?	
Behaviour	What **will** I do?	

4.6 STRATEGIES FOR HANDLING RESISTANCE TO CHANGE

So far in this chapter, we have considered what you can do to prepare for change in general, to reduce the resistance to specific changes, and how to implement the change process yourself in response to more minor problems or opportunities in the workplace.

However, it is likely that even the best manager will meet with resistance. So what can you do when resistance occurs?

There are six possible general strategies open to managers to handle resistance to change. These are shown below.

Strategy	Definition
1 Education and Communication	Talking, teaching
2 Participation and Involvement	Working together
3 Facilitation and Support	Helping
4 Negotiation and Agreement	Trading
5 Manipulation and Co-option	Influencing
6 Explicit and Implicit Coercion	Using power

ACTION POINT 31

Consider the list of strategies above and think about occasions when you have considered or used each of them in relation to your own team. Jot down examples.

The strategies listed above are given in very much the preferred order of use.

We hope that your natural managerial style and your sense of the company culture will mean that the last of the options are used relatively rarely and only in particular circumstances.

In managing your people, both as individuals and as members of a team, talking, teaching and working together will be the norm of managerial behaviours.

Communicating the idea to your team members of change as an opportunity that brings with it possibilities for self-development (directly or indirectly) will be one aspect of this.

Support and help in change will also be the norm, provided that in helping you do not take the initiative away from the member of staff and stifle their self development, and that you do not as a consequence neglect something else which you should be doing.

Trading is sometimes necessary when implementing change. It may be that resistance can be overcome by an incentive offered at the right time, as long as you are seen to be offering it as a reasonable reward for the efforts that will be needed to cope with change, rather than as a 'bribe'.

Where there is strong resistance to change which must be implemented quickly (in matters perhaps of operational safety) you may have to consider the last options when other ways have failed or appear inadequate. But the use of manipulative or power tactics are to be avoided if at all possible and should not generally be necessary in a team where an open, responsible and trusting climate has been fostered. Resorting to them (unless 'telling' is clearly accompanied by a reasoned explanation of why it is necessary) will quickly destroy your credibility with your team and act against the idea of creating a climate of trust and participation.

ACTION POINT 32

Look back at the range of strategies for dealing with resistance to change. Think back to the example of supervising an inquiry desk, and having to introduce the recording of inquiries by your staff

1   Describe what you think would be the best approach to the situation if you found there was initial resistance to the change.

2   What would be the likely reaction in your view if you used strategies 5 and 6 to begin with?

You will have decided yourself on how far the resistance to the change is taken, but we hope that you would see that best strategy as a combination of the first four approaches, with any further suggestions being seen as applying Only in exceptional circumstances.

Starting off by imposing the change would certainly lead to resentment and a sense of your team's feelings and reactions being of no value or concern. Using manipulation to gain your end would cause you not to be trusted as a manager in the future.

From your answers to this Action Point, it should be apparent that it is better to use the strategies at the top of the list first.

4.7 I'M OK - MY STAFF'S OK

Douglas McGregor's Theory X and Theory Y assumptions about workers in organisations is as follows.

Theory X holds that man is indolent, lacks ambition, is indifferent to organisational needs, and resists change.

Theory Y states that it is organisations that have made people passive, but that 'the motivation, the potential for development, the capacity to assume responsibility, the readiness to direct behaviour towards organisational goals, are all present in people'.

ACTION POINT 33

Complete the following statements with either X or Y, whichever you feel is most likely to be true in each case.

1   My behaviour is mainly _____

2   Staff who work for me are mainly _____

3   Staff think I am mainly _____

4   Staff think of themselves as mainly _____

If you find that you have answered any of these questions with 'X', then discuss your answers with a colleague to see if they agree. It is not unusual for managers to see themselves as 'Y', but to see others as 'X'. Is this likely to be the case?

When you have completed this Action Point, continue with the text.

Change is easiest to achieve when all concerned are working together with the same objectives in mind.

That is the challenge of change which faces you as a manager. You need to

■ identify and satisfy your staff's personal needs as early and quickly as possible

■ show a positive attitude to change personally and show that you confidently expect the best attitude also from your team

■ release their natural motivation to want to be more creative, responsible and productive

■ channel their energies into positive, productive, co-operative areas so that the sense of achievement reinforces the drive to go on

■ communicate clearly to the team how any change relates to the shared corporate goals

CHAPTER SUMMARY

After completing this chapter you should now

■ be aware that the manager has to manage the work team through the period of change

■ understand that the manager has also to cope with his or her own problems of change and responsibility

■ recognise that the manager can exert a powerful personal influence, as well as increasing the team's awareness of the pressures for change

■ recognise that resistance to change can be expected, and that the manager needs to be aware of the best practice and strategies to carry the team positively through change

■ see change as potential opportunity for higher achievement and development within the chapter

If you are unsure about any of these areas, look back and re-read the relevant part(s) of the text.

5 COMMUNICATION AND CHANGE

Change is the testing ground of our management skills, our understanding of people, our honesty and our ability to communicate. If we can manage change successfully then we can be reasonably confident that we can manage routine and continuity even more successful.

The importance of communication in managing change is obvious. Helping people to understand why changes are taking place, supporting them through the transition, solving the problems that arise, getting people involved and committed - all of these are about communication, and we shall be looking at all of them in this chapter.

5.1 SOME STRATEGIES FOR GAINING SUPPORT

The golden rule of 'do as you would be done by' applies here. We all know what it feels like to be kept in the dark and to feel powerless and manipulated, but when we do it to others we expect them to be grateful! These strategies for gaining support for change are, therefore, little more than common sense applied to the premise that other people have much the some feelings as you when they are placed in the same situation.

If people are to support change they have a few simple requirements

- they need the 'big picture', the background and context for the proposed change, and what it is meant to achieve

- they need to be able to visualise themselves and their situation as they will be after the change

- they need to feel that their personal security and esteem is not in doubt

- they need to be involved in the planning and implementation as early as possible

- they need to see change as part of an endless process in which the company seeks continuous improvement in performance, quality, service, competitiveness, cost-effectiveness and so on

In the rest of this chapter we shall look at each of these in more detail.

Background, Context and Purpose

We all need to feel that we understand what is going on around us, that we have a reasonably accurate working model in our heads of how things work and why people do what they do. It is this kind of taken-for-granted understanding which underlies our feeling of belonging, or being at home in our own community, workplace and culture. We appreciate its value only when we can no longer take it for granted, that is, when we find ourselves in a different place or a different culture where our working mould does not apply.

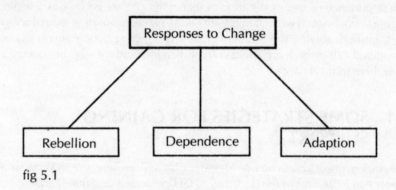

fig 5.1

There are three ways we can react to this, two child-like and one adult. The child-like ways are rebellion and dependence.

Rebellion is about discounting everything that is new and different and insisting that nothing has changed, you are right and everyone else is wrong. Dependence is about being overwhelmed by the new and the different, not even trying to understand, and letting someone else make your decisions for you. You can recognise both these responses in the familiar stereotypes of the Englishman abroad.

The adult response is to construct a new working model of the new situation, by observation, by questioning and, possibly, by trial and error.

Notice that rebellion and dependence are natural reactions to lack of information in a new situation. The adult response of constructing a new understanding is based upon access to information.

It is often said that the first question which people ask about any change is, 'what's in it for me?'. In fact that question is usually no higher than second. The first question is almost invariably 'Why?', and this is a question which has two different kinds of answers

Because   ie. the antecedents, the circumstances and the background

and

In Order to ie. the purposes and intentions.

The first relates to the present situation and what needs to be done, the second relates to the future and what needs to be achieved. As a general rule, people need to appreciate any proposed change from both these perspectives. Vision is not enough, neither is discontent with the present. But if the two can be married together then you have a very powerful source of support.

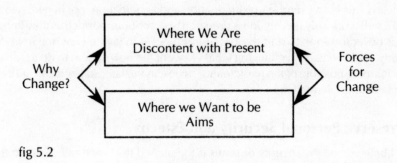

fig 5.2

If you want to make a constructive response to complaints about impending changes, then it is quite a good practice to treat them as requests for explanation. If you can meet a complaint with information, instead of denying or rejecting it, then you have moved the dialogue into more productive territory.

Visualise the New Situation

We have already seen that fear of the unknown is a very powerful motivator and a powerful force of resistance to change. We can deduce from this that the more you can make known the better, because this minimises the area of unknown, and consequently minimises the resistance which is founded upon it.

We cannot literally know the future until we are actually there, but this does not justify us in suspending our judgement indefinitely and asking people to 'wait and see'. We can help to give people a grip on the future and assert some control over it if we can get them to rehearse it in their minds. We can call this 'visualising', but it is not only to the visual sense that we are appealing. 'What will it look, feel, sound, smell like when we are in the new situation?' And for the individual, 'What will I be doing, thinking, using, feeling, learning, saying?' Where and how will I fit in the new situation?

If you can get people involved in this process, really using their imagination to project themselves into the new situation and, so to speak, observing their own reactions to it, then you can generate several useful outcomes at the same time

- identifying in advance some of the barriers that may hinder the acceptance of the change. Some barriers may be only 'in the mind', but they are nonetheless real to the people who express them
- helping to produce plans for implementation
- increasing commitment to the change, because people will have begun to 'own it' on their problem

Clearly this is an exercise in participation and anticipation, not in guesswork, so it will work only if everyone is prepared to contribute as much as they know. It is never too soon to start this process and never to late to continue it. In the early stages it helps in changing what we want the new system to do to satisfy as many as possible of the participants' needs. In the later stages it can address details of implementation.

Preserve Personal Security and Esteem

If I believe that my security or status is threatened then, naturally, I go on the defensive to repel the threat. Conversely, if I am satisfied that, whatever may happen, my security and esteem will be preserved, then I will be prepared to take more risk. To put it another way, a lot of risk will have been taken out of the situation.

This is one of the basic concepts of Japanese management. In large Japanese companies the employees are to assured that the management will not allow the consequences of change to harm their interests, that the staff themselves have become major initiators of change. In Japanese policy of continuous improvement in product and method is based upon an implicit contract that the benefits of change will be shared among all the participants.

By contrast, most employees outside Japan can recall plenty of examples of manipulative change, where all the benefits have gone to one group and all the costs to another. Against this background they are understandably reluctant to collaborate in their own downfall.

Involving People Early

If we are serious about wanting people to be committed to change and supportive, rather than merely compliant, then there are some obvious benefits in getting people involved as early as possible

- it demonstrates trust
- more importantly, it enables people to make their individual contributions to the new developments

The more they can put their mark on it, the more they will own it and make sure that it works.

The opposite is the case where people are not involved in impending change.

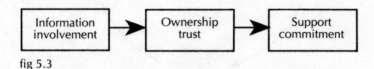

fig 5.3

A classic self-fulfilling prophecy is at work here. The reason managers and managers are reluctant to involve staff in planning changes in the very early stages is that they anticipate objections and resistance. There seems little point in provoking these any earlier than you have to, especially if you feel vulnerable while your plans are only half-baked. In self-defence, managers are often reluctant to reveal their hand until they 'have got their act together' or 'have all their ducks in a row'.

The consequence of all this secretiveness is, of course, the exact opposite of what is intended. When staff are presented with a plan which has reached an advanced stage of preparation and precision they examine it very closely for ways in which it will not work, that is, for defects which could have been avoided if they had been asked earlier. What might have been a helpful suggestion if it could have been made in time, becomes a distinctly unhelpful complaint when it is produced too late to affect the issue.

In this way managers who fail to involve people in decision making, because they fear that progress will be delayed by objections, moans and complaints, persuade themselves that their fears have been justified, when the objections, moans and complaints come out anyway.

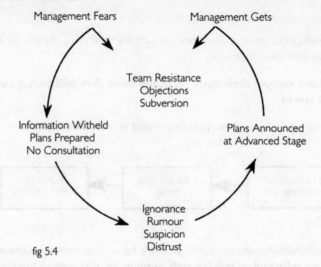

Management Fears   Management Gets

Team Resistance
Objections
Subversion

Information Witheld
Plans Prepared
No Consultation

Plans Announced
at Advanced Stage

Ignorance
Rumour
Suspicion
Distrust

fig 5.4

The way to break out of this vicious circle is obvious, but it still requires courage, because it defies what seem to be the lessons of experience.

Showing the Continuous Process of Improvement

Most people still do not appreciate how profound are the changes that have taken place in business in the 80s and early 90s. There are no more captive markets, there is no more government intervention and regulation to temper the impact of competition, there are no longer any 'unsophisticated' markets where new customers will buy what the old customers no longer want. Customers are increasingly aware that they have a choice, and increasingly they choose to pursue novelty, change and improvement. People expect their next car to be even more automated than their last one. They take it for granted that their new washing machine will be more fuel-efficient, more programmable and nicer looking than their old one. Insurance companies which pay out on the 'replacement value' of damaged stolen goods often have difficulty in deciding what would constitute a 'replacement', when all the goods currently available have features which were not available when the original item was bought.

All of this is so familiar to us as consumers that we do not even stop to think about it. However, the thinking would be very useful to us in our role as producers because the same considerations apply. For every consumer who takes continuous product improvement and development for granted, there has to be a producer who does the same.

'Breakthroughs', revolutions, complete 'rethinks' of our product range will always be very rare events. What keeps us in business is the more mundane work of keeping ahead of the competition. Keeping a lead does not mean being out of sight. It is sufficient to be just for enough ahead to be first past the post. This implies on endless, restless search for improvement in whatever ways we can think of: quality, quantity, delivery, reliability, responsiveness, timeliness, cost-effectiveness and so on.

Obviously, in the constant search for improvements large and small, the more people you involve in the research the more improvements you will find. But even if people are not actively involved in seeking improvements at least they need to be sympathetic to the idea of continuous improvements. The best way of establishing such sympathy is to demonstrate how any particular change will constitute an **improvement**.

ACTION POINT 34

1   Make a list of 'product improvements' in your area of work over however many years you wish to consider

2   What was the staff's response at the time to the changes which you have just listed? How do you account for these responses?

5.2   MANAGING THE TRANSITION

Ultimately there can be no change unless people are involved in ways and means.

In effect, that summarises the theme of this whole unit. Sooner or later everyone has to be brought on board. We have argued that sooner is better than later, so that you can use the energy and ideas of the many to move faster and further than would be possible otherwise.

However, you can involve people in different ways, and more or less deeply. The recurring decision which you have to make is, what kind of involvement is appropriate in each particular case, or at each stage in the change programme.

Where are you going to position yourself along this scale?

| Sharing Information | Clarifying Purposes and Problems | Joint Decision Making |

fig 5.5

The further to the right you are on this scale the more commitment you will have, and the less control. The further to the left you go the more control you retain. The sensible policy would seem to be to start in the middle, and be prepared to move rightwards of leftwards depending on what sort of information emerges.

The STP Technique of Discussion

There is a useful technique for doing this, which enables you to manage what might otherwise be a freewheeling and inconclusive discussion, and to impose some order and logic on it without suppressing free speech.

It is a variation on Brainstorming, where all ideas and suggestions are recorded as soon as they are raised, without any editing or criticism. Any evaluation is left till later.

The conventional logic of discussion about change is that

- you begin by defining where you want to be

- you then review where you are

- and finally, you decide how you are going to make the transition

Unfortunately, life is rarely as neat as that, and, in discussing change, ideas, information, suggestions, aims and problems tend to come out in almost any order, as they occur to the participants. If you try too hard to impose some formality and logic on the discussion you are liable to inhibit people and lose a number of potentially valuable contributions. The technique is to accept contributions as they come, in whatever order, but to record in their logical order for review later.

Every contribution has to fall into one of three categories

■ it is a statement about the present **Situation**, ie. where we are now

■ it is a statement about our **Target**, ie. where we want to be

■ it is a **Proposal** ie. a suggested action to help make the transition

If you were conducting a discussion you could use a board divided into three columns, or set up three flip-chart sheets, labelled thus

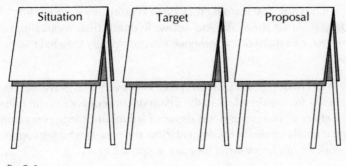

fig 5.6

As each contribution is made you record it under its appropriate heading. When the flow of contributions has dried up you can review what you have, and establish the links across the three chapters.

■ every **Proposal** for action should link back to a **Target** (it should be directed at **achieving** something)

■ every **Situation** should be related to a **Target** (we are not interested in describing how things are, unless there is something we want to do about it)

■ every **Target** must link in both directions (we have no chance of getting where we want to be without knowing how that differs from where we are now, and taking some action to bridge the gap)

By reviewing our STP lists in this way, we can fill in some of the missing links, and eliminate the irrelevant (unlinkable) items, until we have a consistent picture of what needs to be done and why, to achieve the transition which is under review. Then, we can decide who should do what, and how.

The neat feature of STP is that you can use it in several different ways. As we have seen, if you are leading a discussion, you can use STP to give the discussion a useful structure without using a heavy hand to control contributions. You can also use it to take your own notes, if you are a member of group discussing change; you can use these to help the group move forward. Finally, you can use it to help you make sense of opinions, information and ideas which you gather by speaking to individuals.

5.3 HELPING PEOPLE TO LEARN NEW SKILLS AND ROLES

All change will involve some learning. It would hardly deserve to be called 'change' if it did not. The learning may be to acquire any combination of new knowledge, skills or roles. As you know, learning (like motivating) is not something you can do to or for someone else; ultimately they have to do it for themselves.

Your role is to encourage and aid this process in every way possible, because it is potentially the weakest link in the chain of consequences which leads to successful change. The commonest cause of failure in change programmes is that, when it finally comes to implementation, the people who are supposed to make it work do not know what they are supposed to do.

There are many reasons why it is easy to overlook the need to make provision for learning

■ the schedules for change are most frequently based upon 'hard' technical factors, like the delivery time for new equipment or the time required to rearrange work areas. The lead time required for the staff to learn their parts is regarded, by comparison, as a 'soft' factor, which can be moulded to fit around the 'hard' ones

■ very often what needs to be learned does not become clear until most of the 'technical' decisions have been made and the design of the new system is substantially complete. By the time most of the technical requirements of the change are in place there is a strong pressure to go ahead and launch the new way as quickly as possible. The lead time for learning is then seen as 'delaying the implementation' rather than as an essential stage in that process

■ learning new ways puts additional pressure on the time and attention of staff; especially if it takes place while they are still keeping the old system going

As a result of all this, learning is often left to the last minute, and then rushed through. Staff then go into the new situation feeling ill-prepared and guilty, with predictable consequences.

How can you prevent this scenario in your area?

The first requirement is simply to be alert to the possibility of it happening. There are also some specific steps you can take

■ make sure that learning time is built into the considerations of whoever is planning and managing the change, keep asking them: 'What will people have to do differently? 'How will they learn that?' When are they going to be given the time?'

■ keep yourself up to date on what is being planned, and inform your staff as early as possible of what is expected of them

■ spread the learning. Divide it into small digestible steps rather than accumulate it until it becomes a major project

■ relate the new to the old. Go from the known to the unknown. Contrive successful experiences for people in learning whatever new skills are required

■ use a systematic framework for categorising what needs to be learned. One such framework, for example, is

Goal- 'This is what we are trying to achieve'

Data- 'This is where information will come from - This is what it will look like - This is what it will mean?'

Role - 'This is where you will fit in'

Method - 'This is how we will do things'

Criteria - 'These are the standards by which we will be judged - This is how we will know if we have succeeded'

You can use these labels to identify where any particular briefing or discussion fits into the overall picture, and to help your staff to assimilate information or to contribute ideas in a piecemeal fashion. You can also use the framework to check whether your picture is complete, and to identify what else you and your staff need to know. It is like painting by numbers.

ACTION POINT 35

Here are some random extracts from the 'Time Manager' of a manager in a department which is going through a major transition. Identify what each item is about, in terms of the labels we have described above, ie. Goal, Data, Role, Method, Criteria. Compare your answers with what follows.

1   'see G. about reporting relationships and grading structure for 1990.'

2   'meeting to decide new format for our monthly summary reports.'

3   'brief staff on self-monitoring procedures.'

4   'attend briefing on proposal to reduce turnover time for weekly returns.'

5   'reply to Systems Teams' proposal to supply what they think are more user-friendly displays and print-outs.'

6   'redesign 'ready-reckoner', and rewrite my bit of the 'Organisation Guide'.'

7   'poll the opinions of staff on norms for timekeeping and turn-round of correspondence.'

8   'meeting on 'beating the competition.'

Arguably some of the items fall into more than one category, but we think that they are primarily

1   Role

2   Method

3   Method (note: the work 'Procedures' identifies this activity as being about method rather than **criteria)**

4   Goal (possibly method?)

5   Data

6   Data

7   Criteria

8   Goal

Use Change to Develop Individuals

In times of change there is more work to be done: decisions, plans, designs, tests, investigations, negotiations. All of these are time-consumers over and above the normal work load; but, you can choose to view them as opportunities as well as threats. It depends on what spectacles you are wearing.

Viewed as opportunity, the additional workload created by change allows people to

- sample new tasks
- find out how effective they are in new situations
- generally stretch themselves and their horizons

Since you will usually be dealing with tasks and situations which will not repeat themselves in the same form, it becomes possible to take on new tasks or roles on a trial basis, without any permanent commitment.

The period of change can then become a sort of laboratory for developing new skills and new perspectives, and for discovering talents which were previously unused. Once you see it this way it is fairly easy to see ways to take advantage of the situation.

ACTION POINT 36

Note briefly at least 3 ways in which you can use the opportunities provided by change to expand the abilities of your staff.

The possibilities are huge, if not infinite, so we will not try to guess what you have put on your list, or suggest the 'right' answers. Instead, we shall discuss four of the more obvious ways.

Allowing Choices

It would be pretentious to call this 'delegating decision-making' but that is what it is, in effect. Many of the choices and decisions which have to be made are of the kind which can with benefit be delegated to the people who will have to implement them if

■   the choice is a matter of implementation rather than policy or principle

■   it could benefit from the practical experience of the staff

■   it is important to have the commitment of staff to the decision

■   you are willing to stand by whatever decision is made

When any of these conditions obtain then it is worth considering delegating the decision. And just to make sure that it is indeed a learning experience, ask your staff members to review with you how they set about the task. This is not so that you can veto it, or amend it, or take back what you have previously given; it is to mark out what they have achieved and how the experience can be carried forward into other situations.

Using Task Forces

Task Forces are used at the very highest level in some companies to initiate and plan major changes. They are ad hoc groups that cut across the boundaries of departments and organisational status. The idea is to gather together those people who can bring the best combination of knowledge, skill and experience to managing the particular job in hand. When the job is done the group is disbanded.

There is no reason why you should not use the same approach in your area of responsibility, or persuade others to use it in way which will involve your staff. Ideally the Task Force will be given responsibility for planning and implementing some well-defined objective. You may not be in a position to set up a group with this level of responsibility; but even if they are used in a mainly advisory or investigatory role the principles can still apply. These are

- assemble a group on the basis of their knowledge, skills and commitment, regardless of section or status

- set them an objective

- let them make their own decisions on how they set about the task

- disband them when the job is done

ACTION POINT 37

Can you see any opportunities for using, or lobbying for this approach in your area?

What tasks would you set them?

Who would you like to see involved?

What are you going to do about it?

Your answers will clearly depend on your job, but you may find it helpful to talk through your ideas with your line manager.

Use Volunteers

'A volunteer is worth ten pressed men.' If there are jobs that need to be done, and if they provide opportunities for learning, then you can draw up a shopping list, and circulate it with a call for volunteers.

The shopping list would need to specify, at least

■   what needs to be done - a list of discrete items

■   what sort of person each item would be suitable for, in terms of their existing knowledge and experience

■   what they would learn as a result of taking on the task - what sort of an opportunity it is

■   how much work would probably be needed - how much of it would be in normal working time

■   what a successful output would look like, with timescales and deadlines

Obviously, the main inducement to buy is the learning opportunity, so you will need to make that very clear, and you may need to enhance it in some way if it is not sufficiently attractive.

Build-in Motivators and Rewards

It is only elementary justice that people who put their time and personal commitment into supporting changes should be recognised and rewarded in some way. Virtue may be its own reward, but it would be a reckless manager who placed complete reliance on this to get the difficult jobs done.

What we are talking about here is not so much a technique as a way of looking at the world, so that you can see opportunities for giving added value to activities which might at first sight appear unrewarding.

Your starting point has to be an acute awareness of what motivates people; what they regard as being rewarding, not in general terms but in specific detail.

ACTION POINT 38

Try a do-it-your yourself brainstorm. How many different motivators can you note down in 6 minutes?

Here is the output of one brainstorm; it lays no claim to being comprehensive

health	more time	money
popularity	looking better	security
praise	comfort	leisure
pride in accomplishment	'getting-on' (at work or in a social context)	self-confidence
autonomy	prestige	admiration
being up-to-date	being creative	influence over others
sociability	being first	being an authority
expressing own personality	being an individual	being independent
satisfying curiosity	being like someone else (an admired other person)	respect
possessions		

There is plenty to choose from here. If you cannot hang some of these values on the tasks you want people to do, then, either you are not trying, or the change really is going to be unmitigated bad news and you might as well stop pretending otherwise.

The classic principle of selling is 'Sell the Benefits of your Product not the Features'. The customers buy what the product can **do for them** not what it **is**.

For example, they buy 'longer intervals between services' rather than 'improved design of engine and transmission', they buy 'easier programme selection' rather than 'integrated micro-processor controls'. As a manager, your staff are your customers. What are they going to buy?

In case you think this all sounds rather cynical, consider that we are talking about **reward** not manipulation. The important thing is to deliver on the promise.

Help People to Make the Break with the Past

People have an emotional need to take their leave of the past in some symbolic or ceremonial way. If we try simply to snatch off the past and pretend it never happened they will be left with an uneasy feeling of 'unfinished business'. The more we try to suppress the past, the more we feel, compelled to keep harking back to it.

Nostalgia, grief, whatever the feeling might be, it needs expression, so that people can discharge the emotion, and set themselves up to face a future that is going to be different. Allow people space for the expression. Hold a party, or a wake, to mark the passing of the old. Make it an identifiable **event**. Only then will you be able to celebrate the new, and direct peoples energy whole-heartedly into making it a success.

CHAPTER SUMMARY

Having completed this chapter you should now

■ understand the value of communicating the reasons for and purposes of change to your team

■ see the usefulness of visualising the future as a technique for identifying barriers and problems, finding solutions and gaining support

■ be aware of the need to involve your people appropriately in the ways and means of change

■ be able to use the STP discussion framework

If you are unsure about any of these areas, go back and re-read the relevant part(s) of the text.

Further Reading

Adams, Hayes and Hopkins   Transitions
Pitman Bath 1974

Burns and Stalker   The Management of Innovation
Tavistock Press London 1966

Child John   Organisation
Harper and Row NY 1984

Coopey et al   Develop Your Management Potential
Kogan Page 1993

Dale M   Developing Management Skills
Kogan Page 1993

Stacey Ralph   Managing Chaos
Kogan Page 1992

Stacey Ralph   Strategic Thinking and the Management
of Change
Kogan Page 1993